300
Incredible
Things for Pet Lovers
on the
Internet

300INCREDIBLE.COM, LLC
600 Village Trace, Building 23
Marietta, Georgia 30067

(800) 909-6505

ISBN 1-930435-03-7

— Dedication —

To my parents, Phil and Arlene Vella, who let me keep any pet that I brought home, and to George, my cockatiel, whom everybody knew.

Bob Vella

To my four-legged best friends—Stormy, Cali and Tutti—who have brought much joy to our family.

Ken Leebow

Introduction

Almost 60 million American households own dogs, cats, fish, birds, reptiles and other small animals. The Internet adds another dimension to loving and caring for pets. Now, you can learn more about your animals in a fun, entertaining and interactive manner. Ask questions, research health issues, shop for accessories and make contact with people and organizations who are concerned with better care for all animals. Happy surfing!

Bob Vella
pettalk@pettalk.com
http://www.pettalk.com

Ken Leebow
Leebow@300INCREDIBLE.COM
http://www.300INCREDIBLE.COM

About the Authors

Bob Vella has been a pet lover all his life and has worked in the pet industry since 1976. He is the host of *Pet Talk America,* a nationally syndicated radio show which airs in over sixty markets, is on the Internet at several pet-related sites (including his own) and on cable. Check your local listings or e-mail Bob to find out how to get the show in your town.

Bob is a true advocate of animal welfare and takes a logical approach to tackling tough issues. He currently shares his home with Shirley, two cats named Simba and Sammi, several fish and Rosie the female tarantula.

Ken Leebow has been involved with the computer business for over twenty years. The Internet has fascinated him since he began exploring it several years ago, and he has helped over a million readers utilize its resources. Ken has appeared frequently in the media, educating individuals about the Web's greatest hits. He is considered a leading expert on what is incredible about the Internet.

When not online, you can find Ken playing tennis, running, reading or spending time with his family. He is living proof that being addicted to the Net doesn't mean giving up on the other pleasures of life.

Acknowledgments

Putting a book together requires many expressions of appreciation. We do this with great joy, as there are several people who have played vital roles in the process. We especially want to thank:

- Our families for being especially supportive during the writing of the book.

- Paul Joffe and Janet Bolton, of *TBI Creative Services,* for their editing and graphics skills.

- Mark Krasner and Janice Caselli for sharing our vision of the book and helping make it a reality.

- The multitude of great people who have encouraged and assisted us via e-mail.

The Incredible Internet Book Series

300 Incredible Things to Do on the Internet

300 More Incredible Things to Do on the Internet

300 Incredible Things for Kids on the Internet

300 Incredible Things for Sports Fans on the Internet

300 Incredible Things for Golfers on the Internet

300 Incredible Things for Travelers on the Internet

300 Incredible Things for Health, Fitness & Diet on the Internet

300 Incredible Things for Auto Racing Fans on the Internet

300 Incredible Things for Self-Help & Wellness on the Internet

300 Incredible Things to Learn on the Internet

300 Incredible Things for Home Improvement on the Internet

300 Incredible Things for Seniors on the Internet

300 Incredible Things for Pet Lovers on the Internet

300 Incredible Things for Women on the Internet

America Online Web Site Directory
Where to Go for What You Need

TABLE OF CONTENTS

TABLE OF CONTENTS (continued)

CHAPTER I
BEST IN SHOW

1
Pet Talk America

http://www.pettalk.com
Start with Bob Vella's site. You can listen to Bob's nationally syndicated radio show, chat with other pet lovers and learn more about your pet.

2
Pet Education

http://www.peteducation.com
You'll find hundreds of articles that will help you enable your pets to live longer and healthier lives.

3
Pet Community

http://www.acmepet.com
From dogs to reptiles, you'll find detailed information, tips, message boards, chat rooms and more.

4
Got Information?

http://www.pet-net.net
Whether you're looking for fellow pet enthusiasts, information about care, breeders or pet supplies, you're sure to find it here. They'll even design a pet Web site for you.

5
Pogo Pet

http://www.pogopet.com
Health, trivia, pet experts, a question of the day and more can be found here at PogoPet.

6
Pets in Cyberspace

http://www.cyberpet.com
This site provides important and useful information—all in a unique and fun manner—for both the pet layman and the experienced pet fancier.

7
Pet Neighbors

http://www.petjam.com
Join the neighborhood. Eileen Gagliano has an interesting article every day and many resources to help in the day-to-day care of your loved one.

8
World of Pet Care

http://www.waltham.com
If it flies, swims or runs, you'll find helpful information about it here.

9
Get the Scoop

http://www.animalnews.com

News, stories and message boards about animals and pets are a click away.

10
Fancy Publications

http://www.animalnetwork.com

This well-known magazine publisher offers information on birds, reptiles and everything in-between. Read current news and articles about your favorites.

11
Searching for Animals

http://www.animalsearch.galganov.net

This animal specific search engine has them listed, from bears to zebras. Of course, you'll find the animals that are most appropriate to bring home.

12
Join the Project

http://www.thepetproject.com
From contests to asking the experts, you'll find many great resources for pet lovers here.

13
Pet Choices

http://www.personalogic.com
http://www.selectsmart.com
http://freezone.com/kclub/purfpets/quiz.html
Making the right choice of new family member can be difficult. Answer a few questions at these sites, and you should get the best pet.

14
All Pets

http://www.allpets.com
Humans need a petcyclopedia with such interesting categories as "Single Pet People" and "Pet Flicks." All the major pets have their own sections.

15
Good News for Pets

http://www.goodnewsforpets.com
If you want to learn what's new in the pet industry or vet community, here's good news for you.

16
Out of This World

http://www.petplanet.com
Name a pet, and you'll find a library of information about it. Get breed details, advice and the latest breakthroughs in pet health products.

17
American Pet Products

http://www.appma.org
If you hear pet statistics in the news, the numbers probably came from this organization. This site provides a "Pet Owner's Manual" and offers great information about industry developments.

18
The Animal and Human Bond
http://www.deltasociety.org
This society's goal is to promote mutually beneficial relationships between animals and people to help people improve their health, independence and quality of life.

19
Animals Healing People
http://www.create-a-smile.org
The human/animal bond has been proven to increase the recovery rate of patients from a variety of physical and psychological impairments.

20
A Place for Pets
http://www.petplace.com
Information for many different animals about care, wellness, training, illness and the human bond is discussed here.

21
Animal Farm

http://www.animalfair.com

This site says, "We're dedicated to a vital and enriching bond between humans and animals. Our mission is to present hip, broad-ranging and entertaining content about pets, animals and people who love them—from the ordinary to the extraordinary."

22
CAN

http://www.pawprints.com

The Canadian Animal Network is dedicated to caring for the animal kingdom.

23
Pet Source

http://www.petsource.com

From pet health to news, you'll find this to be a good source for information.

24
Pet Station
http://www.petstation.com
This site provides an eclectic mix of information on all pets. If you're grieving from the loss of a pet, it even has a phone number for you to call.

25
Women and Pets
http://www.ivillage.com/pets
http://www.women.com/family/pets
From chats to tips, these are places for females who love their pets.

26
Pet Heroes
http://www.petheroes.com
Ilonka Sjak-Shie has been kind enough to develop this online pet community, which unites pet lovers from all over the world and demonstrates that every pet is a hero.

27
Pet Forum

http://www.petsforum.com
Join the forum so you can learn and chat about your pets.

28
Cloning Anyone?

http://www.missyplicity.com
http://www.savingsandclone.com
See Spot. See Spot again and again. This site offers the latest information on the development of the cloning process.

29
Greetings

http://www.acmepetcards.com
http://www.bluemountain.com
Send your favorite pet lovers e-mail greeting cards to brighten their day.

30
Pet Magazines
http://www.magportal.com/c/pets
This portal has a lot of interesting articles from many different publications on the Net.

31
Reading is Fun
http://www.tfh.com
http://www.twodogpress.com
http://www.voyageurpress.com
There are plenty of titles to satisfy your need to know more about your pet.

32
Pet Loss

http://www.foreverpets.com/FP-Petloss.html
http://www.dogheaven.com
http://www.rainbowsbridge.com
http://www.in-memory-of-pets.com

If your pet has died, you've lost a joyful part of your life. These sites will help during your time of grief.

33
Picture This

http://www.petoftheday.com

Every day, this site presents a new pet photo and story to illustrate how animals enrich the lives of people. Send them your pet's information; it could become a "Pet of the Day."

34
Pet News

http://www.backwire.com
Backwire calls it "Order from Chaos" and will e-mail you newsletters and timely articles about subjects you are interested in (e.g., pets).

35
Animal Forum

http://go.compuserve.com/animals
This is the place to discuss your favorite animals, whether they are domestic pets or wild.

36
Pet Sitters

http://www.petsit.com
http://www.petsitters.org
http://www.petsitters.com
Going out of town and need to find a reputable person to take care of your pets? These sites are good starting points.

"You're loyal, eager to please, and willing to work like a dog. You could be a top executive if you didn't bark every time a phone rings."

37
411 = Information

http://www.411pets.com
Ask the vet, find a special breed, buy a pet gift and check out pet events around the country.

38
Join the Forum

http://www.vin.com/petcare
From message boards to newsletters, this pet site is ready to communicate and inform.

39
Virtual Pets

http://www.petz.com
Dogz and Catz are virtual Petz that live on your computer's desktop. Watch where you step!

40
The New York Pets

http://www.nycpetinfoline.com
From adoptions to veterinarians, this site is for New York City residents.
Cities and states everywhere should use this as a model for pet care.

41
Links Galore

http://www.petlinks.com
This one offers a variety of links to pet sites and organizations, including some
about animals that aren't really pets at all—camels, for instance.

42
The First Pet

http://www.whitehouse.gov/WH/kids/html/pets.html
Learn about the many pets that have resided at 1600 Pennsylvania Avenue.

43
All in the Family

http://www.petspartofthefamily.com
Gary Burghoff, of M*A*S*H fame, shares his love of animals with you. You'll be able to ask questions, get tips and send pet postcards. It even has an area just for kids.

44
Travel Companion

http://www.travelpets.com
http://www.petswelcome.com
http://www.petvacations.com
http://www.petsonthego.com
http://www.travelingdogs.com
http://www.companimalz.com
Don't leave home without them. Before you hit the road, read about pet friendly accommodations.

45
Pets and Planes

http://www.air-transport.org
Visit the ATA's Pet Travel Guidelines site, which is designed to assist you in safely transporting your pet by air.

46
The Funnies

http://www.notinmybackyard.com
Dale Taylor has a new cartoon for you to see each day, by visiting the site or subscribing to receive it by e-mail.

47
Join the Group

http://www.egroups.com/dir/Recreation/Pets
Join an e-mail group to share your interests and exchange ideas.

48
Pet Know How

http://www.ehow.com
In the "HOW TO:" box, type in "pets" and you'll be in the know.

49
Ask the Experts

http://www.askme.com
http://www.expertcentral.com
http://www.allexperts.com
Have questions about any pet or animal? These experts will answer.

50
Ask…

http://www.askjeeves.com
… and you shall receive great information in response to your pet questions.

CHAPTER II
HEALTHY MEANS HAPPY

51
Pet Safety

http://www.familysafety.com

Is your pet's world truly safe? How can you prevent dog theft? What'll happen if your pet gets lost, and you can't be reached? Here's a safe bet: you'll get the answers here.

52
First Aid

http://www.petpak.com
http://www.medipet.com

Traveling with your pet? These kits may come in handy.

53
Health and Care Magazine

http://www.petview.com

Petview is your online magazine dedicated to pet health and overall care.

54
Pet Insurance

http://www.ppins.com

http://www.pethealthinsurance.com

Pet insurance can cover your pet when accident or illness strikes, and protect you from the high cost of quality veterinary care.

55
Poison Control

http://www.napcc.aspca.org

In an animal's life-or-death situation, these folks can assist. To be prepared, you might want to visit before there is a problem.

56
Animal Medical Health Assistance

http://www.animalcareusa.org

The Animal Care Foundation will teach you how to start your own local medical and rescue aid affiliate agency.

57
Vets and Pets

http://www.avma.org

This home of the American Veterinary Medical Association has great news stories and pet health care tips. Kids should be sure to click on the "Kid Korner" section.

58
Vet Info

http://netvet.wustl.edu
http://netvet.wustl.edu/ssi.htm
These vet sites cover everything from finding a veterinary hospital in your hometown to job listings for veterinarians and vet techs. Great health tips for pets are also included.

59
Veterinarian Community

http://www.vetcentric.com
http://vetmedicine.about.com
These sites provide veterinary advice, an encyclopedia, information about diseases and much more.

60
Healthy Pet

http://www.healthypet.com
Your link to the American Animal Hospital Association, this site features an informative library and can help you find a veterinarian in your community.

61
Just a Minute

http://www.animalinstincts.com
Listen to a one-minute broadcast about health issues of dogs, cats and other animals.

62
How Much to Eat?

http://www.petsmart.com/pfc/foodcalc
Here's a calculator to help you determine how much food your pet should consume. This tool has become an industry standard and is the result of considerable research published in scientific journals.

63
Purina

http://www.purina.com
http://www.dogchow.com
In addition to all of its food products, Purina has many articles about health care and general tips.

64
Premium Pet Food

http://www.hillspet.com
Many veterinarians recommend Hill's pet food. Learn the story behind this very popular brand.

65
Iams

http://www.iams.com
Read through this site, and you will know which food is right for your pet. You can find many informative articles and even learn when your pet is considered a senior citizen.

66
Back to Basics
http://www.backtobasicspetfood.com
Discover an alternative pet food that has all natural ingredients and follow news that affects the pet food industry.

67
Holistic Alternatives
http://www.alternativesforanimals.com
Here are holistic alternatives in pet care and pet products. You can even find an animal communicator that can tell you where your pet hurts.

68
Cat Care
http://www.shojai.com
Amy Shojai is one of the most prolific pet book writers in America. At her Web site, you can investigate new books and pet care tips.

69
Bugged Pets
http://www.programpet.com
Flea control is very important to the health and well-being of your pet. Read how this pill breaks the flea's life cycle.

70
Tooth Fairy
http://www.petdental.com
An astounding 80% of dogs and 70% of cats show signs of oral disease by age three. Grab a toothbrush and go to this site.

71
Vet Magazine
http://www.dvmnewsmagazine.com
Read what the vets read. There is a special section for pet lovers, including news stories.

"You're so thin...are you a model?"

72
On Key (and No Fleas)
http://www.nofleas.com
Learn about Advantage, Bayer's answer to flea control. Is your pooch musical?
Check out how to enter the contest for North America's Best Singing Pet.

73
Join the Revolution
http://www.revolutionpet.com
Here's Pfizer's new topical parasiticide for dogs and cats. Learn about other
medications that your vet might prescribe.

74
Your Vet and You
http://www.vetmall.com
At this mall, you will be able to keep up with the latest information about pets,
livestock, new medicines and great animal care products.

75
Veterinarian Schools
http://www.horse-country.com/vet/schools.html
Want to be a veterinarian? Here is a complete list of schools. Start studying!

76
Vet Jobs
http://www.darwood.ca/vetjobs
Looking for a job working with animals? Whether veterinarian or entry level position, this site has listings from around the country.

CHAPTER III
GIMME SHELTER

77
Sherlock Bones

http://www.sherlockbones.com
Tracer of missing pets, Sherlock has been on the beat for more than twenty years and can help find yours.

78
Lost and Found

http://www.pmia.com
Let's hope you don't need this site, but if you do, Pets Missing in Action will allow you to post a lost and found ad at no charge.

79
Missing Pets

http://www.missingpets.com
This site features a nationwide database for lost and found pets.

80
Help 4 Pets

http://www.help4pets.com
Losing a pet is very traumatic, and having this recovery team to back you up helps a lot.

81
Thousands of Pets

http://www.petfinder.org
Petfinder has over 12,000 animals to adopt from over 1,000 shelters. Check out the variety of animals and breeds.

82
Save Our Strays

http://www.saveourstrays.com
"The great aim of humane education is not only knowledge but action. We must all strive to impart the necessary knowledge to pet caretakers to ensure responsible animal management both in our homes and in our communities."

83
Adopt a Pet

http://www.thepuppycam.com
This site features shelters from around the country with live puppy cams showing pets who need loving homes.

84
Directory of Shelters

http://www.1888pets911.org
The goal here is to provide a nationwide network of all animal welfare agencies.

85
S.F. Live

http://www.sfspca.org
Of all the cities in the United States, only San Francisco currently guarantees that no adoptable dog or cat will be euthanized.

86
National No-Kill Shelter

http://www.hua.org
Hearts United for Animals is a "no-kill" national shelter for dogs and cats. You can view photos of the residents and download an adoption application online.

87
Maddie's Fund

http://www.maddies.org
Community by community, Maddie's Fund intends to spend more than $200 million to help build a No-Kill Nation.

88
Shelter Me!

http://www.aspca.org
This famous organization promotes humane principles, prevents cruelty and alleviates pain, fear and suffering of animals through nationwide information, awareness and advocacy programs.

89
Best Friends

http://www.bestfriends.org
Here's the nation's largest sanctuary for abused and abandoned cats, dogs and other animals.

90
Rescue Me!

http://www.k9central.com
http://www.akc.org/breeds/rescue.cfm
Looking to rescue a purebred pooch? These sites have complete listings of Breed Rescue organizations around the country.

91
All Animal Rescue

http://www.h4ha.org
http://www.creatures.com/StateGuide.html
These sites are dedicated to finding good homes for animals in need.

92
Animal Rights

http://www.peta-online.org
At the online home of People for the Ethical Treatment of Animals, read action alerts about issues that are important to this controversial organization.

93
Let's Be Humane

http://www.hsus.org
The Humane Society of the United States' site is full of information about legislation, shelters and international efforts related to the struggle for the humane treatment of animals.

94
Animal and Child Protection

http://www.americanhumane.org
The American Humane Association is the nation's only national organization dedicated to child and animal protection. Many child abuse laws originated from existing animal laws.

95
Animal Protection Institute
http://www.api4animals.org

This organization is dedicated to informing, educating and advocating the humane treatment of all animals.

96
National Animal Interest Alliance
http://www.naiaonline.org

Its stated mission is to promote a more abundant life for all the people of this planet through a wise and compassionate human relationship with animals and the environment.

97
Stamp Out
http://www.palc.org

You can support a postage stamp to remind us that we need to have our pets spayed and neutered.

98
About Animal Rights
http://animalrights.about.com
Take this course by reading about Animal Rights 101.

CHAPTER IV
CREATURE COMFORTS

99
<u>Go Shopping</u>

http://www.pets.com

Visit the home of the famous sock puppet. He wants you to purchase all of your pet items here, from apparel to vitamins.

100
<u>Superstores Online</u>

http://www.petco.com

http://www.petsmart.com

Two of the biggest brick-and-mortar superstores for pets also allow you to click and order.

101
Easy Shopping

http://www.petopia.com
http://www.petquarters.com
From getting advice to purchasing pet supplies at great prices, these sites can be your headquarters.

102
Shop till You Drop

http://www.drsfostersmith.com
http://www.valleyvet.com
http://www.jbpet.com
http://www.petwhse.com
http://www.petmarket.com
Not as well known as other online stores, these pet supply outlets offer free advice and many products at discount prices.

103
Feed Me

http://www.petclick.com
http://www.petfooddirect.com
At these efficient sites, pet food and more are just a click away.

104
Pet Pharmacy

http://www.internetpets.com
Go here when your pet needs a prescription.

105
Pet Jewelry

http://www.petjewelry.com
This is definitely for the pet that has everything.

GLASBERGEN

"I just called to say I love you.
Oh, it's you...put the cat on the phone."

106
Unique Gifts

http://www.petpro.com
You'll find an amazing array of animal-themed gifts, collectibles and other unique items for humans.

107
Join the Club

http://www.afc-petclub.com
Save on pet care products and services, where "your pet is their pet project."

108
Find a Store

http://www.petindustry.com
Locate pet stores in your area, learn about upcoming trade shows and find out about new legislation that could prevent you from owning pets.

109
Pet Products

http://www.stjon.com
http://www.hagen.com
http://www.fourpaws.com
http://www.dockruger.com
These pet product manufacturers have plenty to offer.

110
Bigdogs

http://www.bigdogs.com
This fun, offline store also has all of its cool dog wear and accessories online.

111
Shop Like a Dog

http://www.decidedlydogs.com
Here are some interesting and fun toys for you and your dog.

112
Toys

http://www.dogtoys.com
Purchase the newest and neatest dog toys — breed-specific, all sizes, ones that squeak and even some that brush teeth.

113
Rock On

http://www.kongcompany.com
Has your dog ever chewed on rocks? That's what helped start this unique dog toy company.

114
Dress Up

http://www.dogsdayout.com
Add a finishing touch to your dog's wardrobe — a nice tie or bow tie should do.

115
Messy Eater?

http://www.smartbowl.com
Does your dog eat like a pig? It won't with the "spill-less smartbowl."

116
Fat Cat

http://www.fatcats.com
What do Newt Hoot, Nasty Neighbor Kid, Toss Perot and Vet the Victim have in common? They are all toys that your cat will love to beat up.

117
Cat Lover Gifts

http://www.marketplaza.com/cats/cats.html
Get your delightful cat gifts here.

118
13 Cat Street

http://www.13cats.com
From accessories to housewares, this site has it. It's the ultimate cat-a-log.

119
House Cat

http://www.housecat.com
This online catalog of useful and unique cat items also has a brief tip section that you should read.

120
Cat Toys

http://www.cattoys.com
Identify toys by breed or personality by using the search feature. Your cat will love you for it.

121
Cat Collectibles
http://www.teleport.com/~tyberk
Get hand-carved collectibles for cat owners here.

122
Pet Drivers License
http://www.chloecards.com
Your pet can have his own driver's license ID card, and he doesn't even have to take the test.

123
Unique Cat Litter
http://www.petecology.com/products.htm
Urinary tract infections are a major concern for cat lovers. This cat litter will alert you by turning pink if your cat has this problem.

124
Pet Odor

http://www.learn2.com/09/0961/0961.asp
This site provides step-by-step instructions on how to get rid of the worst pet messes and gives advice on how to address the issue with your pet in a positive way. You can also purchase one of the recommended products.

125
Chew on This

http://www.kaytee.com
This popular bird food manufacturer also provides an educational avian center for learning more about birds and small animals.

126
Bird Toys

http://www.birdtoys-n-more.com
http://www.birdhous.com
http://www.smartbirdtoys.com
Birds get bored. Check these sites out to keep your pet happy and healthy.

127
Pharmaceuticals for Fish
http://www.aquariumpharm.com
Fish have certain needs, and this colorful site offers information about its products dedicated to them.

128
Tetra
http://www.tetra-fish.com
These people are dedicated to producing quality products and books for the care of aquariums, ponds and terrariums. While you're at the site, create your own Virtual Aquarium.

129
Reef Tanks
http://www.reefs.org
This online home for reef keepers is filled with great information. You have to know what you're doing to keep a reef alive and healthy, so do your homework.

CHAPTER V
RUFF LIFE

130
Wild About Dogs

http://www.dogomania.com
http://www.dogseek.com
Here are search engines and much more for people who love dogs.

131
New Dog

http://www.newpet.com
You'll find fun tips and helpful hints on where to get a pet and how to care for the new addition once you bring your bundle of joy home.

132
Fun Facts

http://www.doghause.com
Here's a virtual playground for dog lovers—fun facts, idioms, art, pet superstitions and much more.

133
Love Your Dog

http://www.howtoloveyourdog.com
This is a kid's guide to dog care.

134
Poop Outside!

http://www.learn2.com/08/0827/0827.asp
Do you need some assistance getting that cute puppy to poop outside?
Here's your helpful learning tool.

135
Purebred
http://www.akc.org
Find out all you ever wanted to know about pedigreed canines and dog shows. Whether you enjoy purebreds, mutts or both, you'll love this informational site.

136
United Kennel Club
http://www.ukcdogs.com
The United Kennel Club was established over 100 years ago and provides a total breed registry.

137
Continental Kennel Club
http://www.ckcusa.com
The Continental Kennel Club is an all breed club that recognizes and registers over 444 known breeds of purebred dogs.

138
Retired Greyhounds

http://www.greyhoundpets.org

This organization of volunteers is dedicated to finding responsible, loving homes for professional racing greyhounds that no longer qualify to compete at the racetrack.

139
Mixed Breeds

http://www.amborusa.org

Mixed breeds have their own registry and competitions, too.

140
Best of Breed

http://www.westminsterkennelclub.org

See the winners of the most famous dog show of all.

141
Rare Breeds
http://www.arba.org
They strive to protect and serve the rare breed dog and serve all dog fanciers.

142
Find the Perfect Breed
http://www.dogbreedinfo.com
Answer a simple survey that will help you find the right dog for your family.

143
It's a Dog's World
http://www.dogworldmag.com
Though the entire monthly magazine is not online, there is a nice Q&A section.

144
Everything Dog

http://www.dog.com
http://www.doginfo.com
http://www.dogsaver.com
Dog news, information, screen savers and more are at these dog sites.

145
Me@Dog.com

http://www.dogmail.com
Want your own e-mail address at Dog.com? Sign up here.

146
Dog Talk

http://www.i-dog.com
This Internet discussion group is an excellent place to ask questions, share knowledge and make new friends.

147
They Do the Digging for You

http://www.pawgear.com
This site's purpose is to dig up as much information on dogs as possible.

148
Stay Awhile

http://www.sitstay.com
Explore current news, comics and products for dogs. Stay awhile; you'll have some fun.

149
Urban Dogs

http://www.urbanhound.com
While designed specifically for pet owners in New York City, any city-dwelling pet owner will enjoy this site.

150
Take a Walk…

http://www.dogpark.com
…in the park, that is. This site lists more than 800 parks in the United States and Canada.

151
Get the Poop on Dogs

http://www.thepoop.com
There are all kinds of fun here. "Shoot the Poop" with other members, visit the Poop Pantry, see some famous "Media Hounds" and more.

152
<u>Traveling With Your Best Friend</u>

http://www.dogfriendly.com
http://www.doggonefun.com
http://www.takeyourpet.com
http://www.traveldog.com

Are you one of the millions of Americans who take vacations with your pets? These sites will help you plan your trip and will give you ideas on where to vacation and stay.

153
<u>Bird Dogs</u>

http://www.fielddog.com

Bird Dog enthusiasts, these grounds are for you. Check out upcoming field trail competitions.

154
Police Dogs

http://www.policedogs.com
See how the professionals train these hardworking public servants.

155
Train Your Dog

http://www.clickerpet.com
http://www.clickertraining.com
Learn training methods that were first used with dolphins. Now your dog can learn just like animals in the entertainment business.

156
Dog Training Tips

http://www.superdog.com
Barking, housetraining, digging and many other situations are discussed here.

157
$10,000 Challenge

http://www.dogproblems.com
Are you a dog trainer? Think you are better at it than Adam Katz? Click on this site and find out the details. The rest of us can also get some good training tips.

158
Dog Crazy

http://www.crazydog.com
Sponsored by five pet manufacturers, this fun site enables you to create personalized greeting cards.

159
Lassie Come Home

http://www.lassie.net
Reminisce and learn the complete history behind the legendary TV dog from the good old days.

160
Blue Dog

http://www.bluedogart.com
The paintings of George Rodrigue have become unbelievably famous.

161
Picture This

http://www.wegmanworld.com
Visit the world of William Wegman, who creates interesting and magnificent photographs of the beautiful Weimaraner.

162
Hang On Snoopy

http://www.snoopy.com
Snoopy changed the life of Charles Schulz and has put smiles on the faces of millions of fans.

163
A Star is Born

http://www.celebritydog.com
If your pooch may have what it takes to be in show biz, then register at this site. Many pets have been discovered here.

164
Puppy Love

http://www.amused.com/puppy
Here's a kiss with an Internet twist.

165
SWF with Dog Seeks Date

http://www.petloversunite.com
Pet-owning singles meet in cyberspace.

166
Name That Dog

http://www.petrix.com/dognames
From Abby to Zeus, there are over 2,000 possible names listed.

167
Deaf Dogs

http://www.deafdogs.org
Sixty-four breeds of dogs are known to have congenital defects that can cause deafness. This group is trying to provide education and funding to improve the lives of deaf dogs.

168
Dogs for the Blind

http://www.guidedogs.com
"We provide Guide Dogs to visually impaired people throughout the United States and Canada. Our dogs and services are free to those we serve, thanks to the generosity of donors and the support of volunteers."

169
Dog Bite Law

http://www.dogbitelaw.com

Have you been bitten by a dog? This site has information you need to protect your rights. Get informative statistics and learn how to prevent bites.

170
Bad Dogs

http://www.baddogs.com

In The Bad Dog Chronicles, Fido and Fifi share their misdeeds with the other Net-connected canines and their masters.

171
PlayDog

http://www.playdog.com

There are great dog pictures and information about all breeds here.

"This is so cool! I'm barking at a cat in Australia!"

172
Be the Top Dog

http://www.tdog.com

When it comes to looking for information about dogs, locating a breeder directory, reading a newsletter or implementing training tips, you've sniffed it out here.

173
Bragging Rights

http://www.infodog.com

If you show dogs, this site is for you. Get up-to-date information on dog shows and which pooches won.

174
Breeder Cup

http://www.dogadvisors.com

Designed for dog breeders, this site also has detailed information for the average dog owner.

175
Vietnam Dog Handlers

http://www.vdhaonline.org
This organization is dedicated to all war veterans who were dog handlers, veterinarians and veterinarian technicians.

176
War Dogs

http://www.war-dogs.com
Learn about how dogs have helped out in wars. These heroic dogs deserve recognition for their involvement, and they get it here.

177
Dog Sled Races

http://www.dogsled.com
http://www.iditarod.com
http://www.sleddogcentral.com
Here's everything you ever needed to know about the famous Iditarod.

178
Big Top Dogs
http://www.great-american-dogshow.com
Come one, come all, and check out this truly unique tribute to dogs. Grab your popcorn and enjoy the show.

179
Doggone Funny
http://www.offthemark.com/dogs.htm
Enjoy Mark Parisi's cartoons about dogs.

CHAPTER VI
BY A WHISKER

180
Best of Show

http://www.cfainc.org
The Cat Fanciers' Association is the world's largest registry of pedigreed cats. Read about the shows, breeds, pet care and more.

181
United, We Stand

http://www.catsunited.com
They are "in relentless pursuit to find the coolest stuff, hot new facts and new information for cats, with cats and about cats."

182
Cat Reference
http://www.sniksnak.com/resources/reference.html
From responsible pet ownership to pet loss, you will find a tremendous amount of good information here.

183
Cute Little Kitties
http://www.cutecats.com
This site has several cute cat games, the cute cat of the day and a cute cat photo tour.

184
Cat Fanciers
http://www.acfacat.com
http://www.fanciers.com
Cat fanciers will find a home at these purrrfect sites that list everything from cat care to cat shows.

185
21 Cats

http://www.21cats.org
Healthcare, fun and games, just for kids, and even a virtual cemetery are at
this site, which has been funded by winnings from the quiz show Twenty-One.

186
Do You Love Cats?

http://www.i-love-cats.com
If you sniff around this site, you will see why people love cats — cat post
cards, cat chat, daily comics and even your own e-mail address.

187
Kitty?

http://www.petrix.com/catnames
Need a name for that new kitten? Here are more than 2,000 possibilities.

188
Use the Litter Box, Please
http://www.learn2.com/08/0886/0886.asp
Does your cat need to learn how to use the litter box? This site will help you with the training process.

189
Grooming 101
http://www.learn2.com/08/0885/0885.asp
Claws getting a little long? Learn how to groom your furry friends.

190
Cat Facts
http://www.petcat.com
Create your own page, and get a virtual cat, news, facts and more.

191
Play Time

http://www.catfaeries.com
From catnip toys to Tarot cards, they're all here for you to buy for your cat or yourself. Feline health products are also included.

192
Bengal Cats

http://www.hdw-inc.com
http://www.bengalcat.com
This is a distinct, unique breed of spotted domestic cat derived from ancestral crossings with an Asian Leopard Cat. This was done in an effort to preserve the stunning beauty of the small forest-dwelling leopard cat as a loving, domestic family pet.

193
Persian Cats
http://www.persian-cats.com
From general information to creating your own Persian Cat Web site, this site will keep you busy and informed.

194
Siamese Cats
http://www.siamesecats.org
Find out more about this highly intelligent breed of cat. Why do they howl?

195
Himalayan Cats
http://www.himalayan.org
This site is for preserving and promoting this wonderful breed of cat.

196
Canadian Cats

http://www.catsincanada.com
You'll find breeders, articles and cat resources available throughout Canada.

197
The UK Cats

http://www.thecatbasket.freeserve.co.uk
http://www.pedigreecat.co.uk
Photos, fun facts, well-known cat lovers, pedigreed cats and even the age of
cats in "human years" can be found here.

198
Crazy for Cats

http://www.catcraze.com
Looking for the cat of your dreams? This site can help. And while you're there,
enter your cat in the photo contest.

199
Feral Cats

http://www.alleycat.org
http://www.feralcat.com
Did you know that a pair of breeding cats, which can have two or more litters per year, could exponentially produce 420,000 offspring over seven years?

200
Traveling Cats

http://www.designltd.com/cats
David Scarbrough travels with his two cats. See these magnificent pictures of the family's trips around the globe.

201
You Can Help

http://www.catwelfare.com
Much work is being done to help cats live longer and healthier lifestyles through medical research.

202
Cat Magazines

http://www.catsandkittens.com
Some of this magazine is available online. The "Amazing Cat Stories" section is guaranteed to bring a smile to any cat owner.

203
I'm a Fanatic

http://www.catfanatics.com
Need to find an unusual gift for your favorite feline lover or a special item for yourself? You've landed in the right place.

204
Toilet Training 101

http://www.rainfrog.com/mishacat/toilet.shtml
Tired of having a litter box around? This site will help you train your cat to use the toilet.

205
Cat Gloves

http://www.softpaws.com
This claims to be "the purrfect solution for problem cat scratching through an effective, safe and humane alternative to declawing."

206
Cat Writers Association

http://www.catwriters.org
Learn about the folks who write about cats.

207
Buy the Book

http://members.aol.com/catsbuzz/STORE.htm
Search through more than 2,000 cat and kitten books by subject.

Einstein's cat.

208
Cats and Water

http://www.catmandrew.com
Welcome to Drew Strouble's gallery, which celebrates the domestic cat. You'll find many beautiful and fun watercolor paintings.

209
Cat of the Day

http://www.catoftheday.com
Is your cat special enough to become the Cat of the Day? Go ahead and enter.

210
Famous Cats

http://www.garfield.com
http://www.felixthecat.com
Visit the official Web sites of these two famous and funny cartoon cats.

211
The Amazing Peanutorio
http://www.peanutorio.com
This superstar cat has starred in such films as "Kung-Fu," "Flying Fists of Fur" and the classic horror movie, "Peanutorio: Terror Has a Name."

212
All About Cats
http://cats.about.com
From adoption to literature and art, these folks have lots of good feline things for you.

213
They're Great!
http://www.greatcatsoftheworld.com
No, these are not the ones that you would normally have in your home, but if you love the big cats, these are some beautiful ones.

214
Cat 'Toon
http://www.offthemark.com/Cat.htm
Enjoy the fun with over a hundred cat cartoons.

CHAPTER VII
FINE FEATHERED

215
Audubon Society
http://www.audubon.org
This organization and Web site have continued the fine work of John James Audubon, the famed ornithologist, explorer and wildlife artist.

216
Searchin' for Birds
http://www.bigbirdsearch.com
Use this bird-specific search engine to find information on the Net.

217
Bird Information
http://www.upatsix.com
Check out avian veterinarians, articles, products, chat groups and frequently asked questions.

218
Avian Vets

http://www.aav.org
If you have parrot-type birds, you may need an avian specialist. Check out this site for answers.

219
Pet Birds

http://www.birdsnways.com
A complete guide to all types of pet birds, you'll find a monthly magazine, shopping, chatting and fun stuff at this site.

220
Bird Brain

http://www.parrotparrot.com
This site puts the love in LoveBirds. Take the quiz to see if you are a birdbrain.

221
<u>Domesticated and Wild</u>

http://birds.about.com
http://birding.about.com
Enjoy detailed reporting and listings for pet birds and the ones in the wild.

222
<u>Bird Watchers</u>

http://www.birdandyard.com
http://www.birdwatchers.com
http://www.birdwork.com
http://www.wildbirdz.com
These sites feature tips on attracting birds to your backyard and offer a large supply of bird equipment, including cages and feeders.

223
Count Birds

http://www.birdsource.org
Want a new hobby? Take part in the great Back Yard Bird Count and keep track of wild birds.

224
Exotic Bird Resource

http://www.toolady.com
Don't let the name fool you. If you are a parrot owner, go here for a great resource on parrot questions.

225
Incredible Talking Bird

http://www.mynahbird.com
Find out about the special needs of mynah birds here. Watch what you say, they learn fast.

226
Rain Forest Bird

http://www.toucan.org
This site is dedicated to people who share an interest in the care, breeding, health and preservation of these treasures of the tropical rain forest.

227
Beautiful Small Birds

http://www.finchworld.com
You might be surprised how many types of finches there are. Be sure to check out the Gouldian.

228
A Different Zebra

http://www.sundgaard.com
This site is designed for everyone who is interested in zebra finches. These little birds are known as "computer birds" because they make a cool chirp that sounds like a computer.

229
Wild Parrots of…
http://www.wildparrots.com
… Telegraph Hill. Learn about the magical relationship with a flock of wild parrots—pets that have begun to breed in the "wilds" of the city.

230
Adopt a Parrot?
http://www.thegabrielfoundation.org
Sadly, many parrots are homeless. This organization will help you adopt a pet parrot and educate you on helping them live a long and happy life.

231
Amazon Pete
http://www.amazonpete.com
Pete—an Amazon parrot, of course—educates people about his particlar breed and about bird care in general.

232
Intelligent Parrot
http://www.africangreys.com
Check out this magical site dedicated to Greys, and learn about the legend of Wart and King Arthur.

233
Planned Parrothood
http://www.plannedparrothood.com
From bird jokes to tips about your parrot, Patricia Barth has created a site for bird parenting.

234
Majestic Macaws
http://www.exoticbird.com
Meet the largest members of the parrot family — the Macaws. This site provides fun and useful information concerning their health and behavior.

235
The Monk

http://www.monkparakeet.com
Be careful with these little birds. They are outlawed in many states for fear that they might become an agricultural menace. This site contains a list of those states in which they are legal.

236
Bird Greetings

http://www.wings-and-things.net
Send a friend a nice bird greeting card by e-mail.

CHAPTER VIII
FIN FARE

237
Giga-Fish

http://www.petfish.com

These downloadable pet fish live in your computer; make sure you feed them.

238
Fish Vet

http://www.koivet.com

This is the most complete koi fish information site available. If you have questions, they have the answers.

239
Aqua Link

http://www.aqualink.com

Here are plenty of links to send you into fish cyberspace.

240
Tropical Fish Digest
http://www.trakkerinc.com/tropfish/tfdintro.htm
From beginners to experts, everyone can learn here.

241
FINS
http://www.actwin.com/fish
Visit the Fish Information Service for a glossary of terms, some answers to frequently asked questions and much more.

242
Public Aquariums
http://fishlinkcentral.com/links/aquariums
http://www.aqualink.com/community/publicaquariums.html
These sites feature links to many popular public aquariums.

"If swimming is good for developing shoulders, arms and legs, why haven't we developed any shoulders, arms and legs?"

243
Fish Resource
http://www.fishlinkcentral.com
From breeders to software, sit back, relax and enjoy the pictures and articles.

244
King of the Aquarium
http://www.discusworld.com
Check out this discus fish hatchery site, and learn exactly how to keep these magnificent fish.

245
Salt Water
http://www.saltwaterfish.com
Everything you need to know about setting up a salt tank is here, answering the major questions for new hobbyists.

246
All-Glass

http://www.all-glass.com
Ever wonder about the tanks we keep our fish in? Learn how they're made and what's new.

247
Fish and Wildlife Foundations

http://www.nfwf.org
http://www.fws.gov
Here's to the love and enjoyment of wildlife.

248
Netscape's Fishcam

http://home.netscape.com/fishcam/fishcam.html
Visit Netscape's legendary fishcam and see what's swimming by.

249
Fish Dance

http://www.fishydance.com

Take a break and watch the fish dance. For some reason, this is one of the more popular sites on the Net. E-mail it to a friend.

CHAPTER IX
REPTILES AND THE REST

250
Herpetology

http://www.herpetology.com
Herpetology is the scientific study of reptiles and amphibians. Start your surfing and studies here.

251
Take Me to the Mall

http://www.reptilemall.com
This mall has it all about reptiles.

252
Iguana

http://www.iguanaden.com
http://www.anapsid.org
These sites will educate and inform you about the Iguana.

253
King of Snakes

http://www.kingsnake.com
Here's "the Internet portal for the reptile and amphibian hobbyist." This site includes the latest news on reptile shows and adoptions.

254
Tons o' Reptiles

http://pages.cthome.net/reptiles
Bearded dragons, blue-tongued skinks, leopard geckos and, of course, snakes—this site has them all.

255
Reptiles and Amphibians

http://www.lpzoo.com/tour/goldtrail/smammal.html
Visit the Lincoln Park Zoo from the comfort of your own computer.

256
Reptile Stuff

http://www.zoomed.com
http://www.flukerfarms.com
http://www.t-rexproducts.com
http://www.tetra-fish.com/reptile.html
These sites are specifically designed for reptile lovers and offer a variety of products for your pet iguana, snake or any other kind of reptile.

257
Outback Reptiles

http://wildlife-australia.com/reptiles.htm
Check out forest dragons, water dragons and brown snakes, all of which are native to Australia.

258
Herpetology and Herpetoculture

http://www.herper.com/Snake.html
What's the difference? This site will explain that and much more.

259
Mice on Ice

http://www.miceonice.com
Find out why nine out of ten snakes prefer mice-icles to other food treats.

260
The Dancing Lizard

http://www.lizarddance.com
Lizards are alive and well and having fun on the Net.

261
Slow Pokes

http://www.tortoise.org
http://www.tortoisetrust.org
If you enjoy tortoises, these sites have plenty of helpful tips and information, including how to get a permit.

262
Tarantulas

http://www.tarantulas.com
Separate the myths from the facts about these misunderstood creatures.

263
Show Bunnies

http://www.showbunny.com
Hop on over to this portal site for information on every type of bunny (and there are more than you thought). See the bunny care section, and send some bunny post cards.

264
Rabbit Society

http://www.rabbit.org
This is a non-profit organization that rescues rabbits and educates the public on rabbit care.

265
Love Those Bunnies

http://www.bunnyluv.com
Get all of your bunny essentials here, including grooming tips, litter boxes and bunny screen savers.

266
Chinchillas

http://www.chin.buffnet.net
Chinchilla lovers can congregate here. From chats to FAQs, you'll find all types of useful information.

267
Furry Rodents

http://www.hamsters.co.uk
This complete hamster site has everything from breeder locators, news and care advice for these furry little pets.

268
Watch 'em Dance
http://www.nuttysites.com/rodent
Train the little ones to dance.

269
Cavies
http://www.cavymadness.com
Tammy says, "Having a piggy companion is a rewarding experience. The extra love and care you give them comes back to you tenfold in cuddles and hours of entertaining antics."

270
Cavies Galore
http://www.caviesgalore.com
A complete site that contains detailed information about pet pigs. You can play fun cavy games and post cavy poetry.

271
Rats and Mice…

http://www.rmca.org
…make great pets. Learn why at this site.

272
Organized Rats

http://www.nfrs.org
The National Fancy Rat Society offers a listing of rat shows, articles and books. Find out the latest in rat care.

273
Gerbils

http://www.gerbils.org
This colorful site offers everything that you need to know about this truly unique pet.

"I never imagined he'd get this big. When we brought him home, we thought he was a guinea pig."

274
Ferrets

http://www.ferret.org
http://www.ferretcentral.org
These pets are gaining in popularity. Learn all about them from these great organizations.

275
Ferrets and Kids

http://www.worldkids.net/critters/pets/exotic/ferrets.htm
Kids can learn about ferret care at this site.

276
This Little Piggy

http://www.pigs.org
http://www.petpigs.com
http://www.pigspeace.org
Read and learn about the highly intelligent and curious nature of pigs.

277
Hedgehogs

http://www.hedgehoghollow.com
http://users.intertex.net/rzu2u/hedgehog.htm
The Hedgehog is defined as "a small, slightly prickly, but utterly adorable Insectivore, with an incredible ability to burrow its way into your heart."

278
Gliding on Sugar?

http://www.sugarglider.com
Even this furry little pet has its own Web site. Check to see if the Sugar Glider is legal in your area.

279
Equine Info

http://www.thehorse.com
http://www.gohorses.com
http://www.equindex.net
http://www.horse-country.com
http://www.horsesamerica.com
These sites offer behavioral and health advice for horse owners and riders
from professionals and veterinarians.

280
Horse Web

http://www.horseweb.com
http://www.horsesense.com
Thinking about buying a horse? Check out these sites for links to breeders'
pages, calendar lists for upcoming horse shows and stables in your area.

CHAPTER X
WONDERFUL WILDLIFE

281
Life is Better with Animals

http://www.animal.discovery.com
Here's the online version of the well-known TV show, "Animal Planet." Make sure you visit the Yelpline, a great place for information to solve some of those daunting pet behavior problems.

282
Animal News

http://www.animalchannel.net
Get the latest, up-to-the-minute news on animals from around the world. All of the stories are delivered via RealAudio.

283
Animal Adventures

http://www.jackhanna.com
Jack Hanna has delighted and entertained us about the animal kingdom for
years on television. Now you can take an exciting journey online to learn about
animals and the places they live.

284
Australian Rainforest

http://rainforest-australia.com
Explore the Australian Rainforest and its teeming plant and animal life.

285
Out of Africa

http://www.africam.com
Can't get there in person? Enjoy Africa with live cameras that can be viewed
from this site.

286
Sea World

http://www.seaworld.org
Check on what's happening at SeaWorld. From seeing Shamu to educational resources, you're sure to be delighted. Clicking on Animal Resources will take you to "Fast Facts" for lots of interesting information.

287
Zoo Fun

http://www.zoobooks.com
Kids can take quizzes, play games and guess what an animal is. There's a section for parents and teachers, too.

288
Our Family

http://www.ourfamilypets.com
Start sharing your pets with friends and family across the globe. Create your personal pet site with photos, text, sound and even video. Best of all, it's free.

289
Interesting Cat Quotes
http://www.bemorecreative.com/tqs/tq-cats.htm
Have fun with great quotes like: "Dogs come when they are called; cats take a message and get back to you."

290
Famous Dog Quotes
http://www.bemorecreative.com/tqs/tq-dogs.htm
Just about everyone has a favorite quote about dogs. Read some of the more famous ones here.

291
Monkey Stock Picker
http://www.monkeydex.com
Quit monkeying around with your own finances, and go bananas over Raven's stock picks. It seems that this monkey can pick stocks better than the pros.

292
Fun Animal Trivia
http://www.funtrivia.com/Animals
Read these interesting facts about animals and have some fun.

293
Wild Animal Trivia
http://www.sunnysafaris.com/guessthe.htm
Test your knowledge about wild animals. Be sure to answer quickly, 'cause you're being timed.

294
African Animal Trivia
http://www.inafrica.com/trivia.htm
Answer trivia questions about these incredible animals from the African continent.

295
How Did You Know?

http://www3.edgenet.net/gaia11/qanimal1.html
http://www3.edgenet.net/gaia11/qanimal2.html
What do folk doctors in the Andes use to detect illness? Snakes? Guinea Pigs? Llamas? Leopards? Go to this site and find out.

296
See If You Win

http://tqjunior.advanced.org/6081/4slb-17.html
This is an interactive animal trivia game. Some questions are easy, but others will test you.

297
Amazing Animal Facts

http://zebu.cvm.msu.edu/~dawsonbr
From dogs to snakes and even a grab bag of facts, you'll find many interesting items here.

298
Stuffed Animals

http://www.stuffed-animals.com
They won't lick your hand, but they sure are cute—no vet bills, either.

299
Pet Encyclopedia

http://encarta.msn.com
http://www.britannica.com
Want to do more research? Go to these superior encyclopedias and search for pets. You'll be propelled to in-depth information about all types of animals.

300
The Hits Keep Coming

http://www.google.com
Have some more time on your hands? Search the Net by topic and spend eons looking at all the sites related to animals. A recent search found 1,419,999 Web pages for "dog," 1,330,000 for "cat," 1,350,000 for "fish," 987,995 for "bird" and 105,000 for "reptile." Happy surfing!

INDEX (BY SITE NUMBER)

Index (by Site Number)

INDEX (BY SITE NUMBER)

The Incredible Newsletter

If you are enjoying this book, you can also arrange to receive a steady stream of more "incredible Internet things," delivered directly to your e-mail address.

The Leebow Letter, Ken Leebow's weekly e-mail newsletter, provides new sites, updates on existing ones and information about other happenings on the Internet.

For more details about *The Leebow Letter* and how to subscribe, visit us at:

WWW.300INCREDIBLE.COM

(USO) United Service Organizations

For nearly 60 years, the United Service Organizations (USO) has "Delivered America" to service members stationed around the world, thousands of miles from family and friends. The USO provides celebrity entertainment, recreation, cultural orientation, language training, travel assistance, telephone and Internet access, and other vital services to military personnel and their families at 115 locations worldwide. The USO is a non-profit organization, not a government agency. It relies on the generosity of corporations and individuals to enable its programs and services to continue. For more information on contributing to the USO, please call 1-800-876-7469 or visit its Web site at www.uso.org.